Illustrated by
MARIE RIVERS

Copyright © 2016 by Marie Rivers

ISBN-13: 978-1541001671
ISBN-10: 1541001672

NNo part of this publication may be reproduced, distributed or transmitted in any form or by any means, without the prior written permission of the publisher, except in the case of brief quotations embodied in critical reviews and certain other noncommerical uses permitted by copyright law.

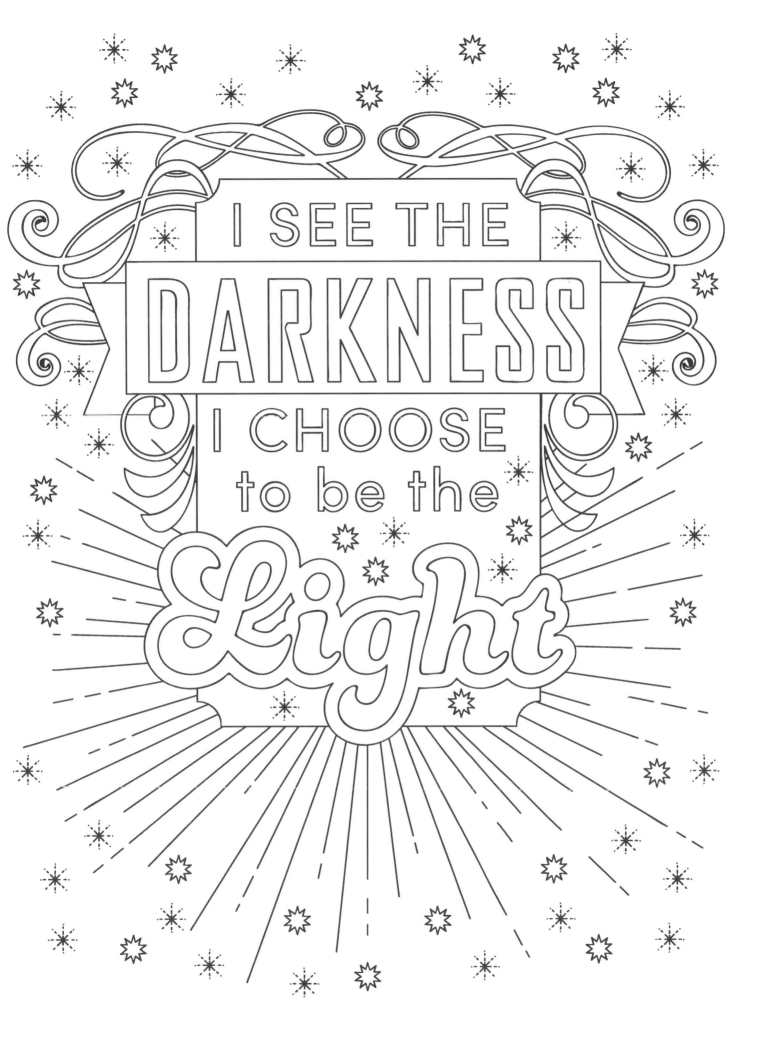

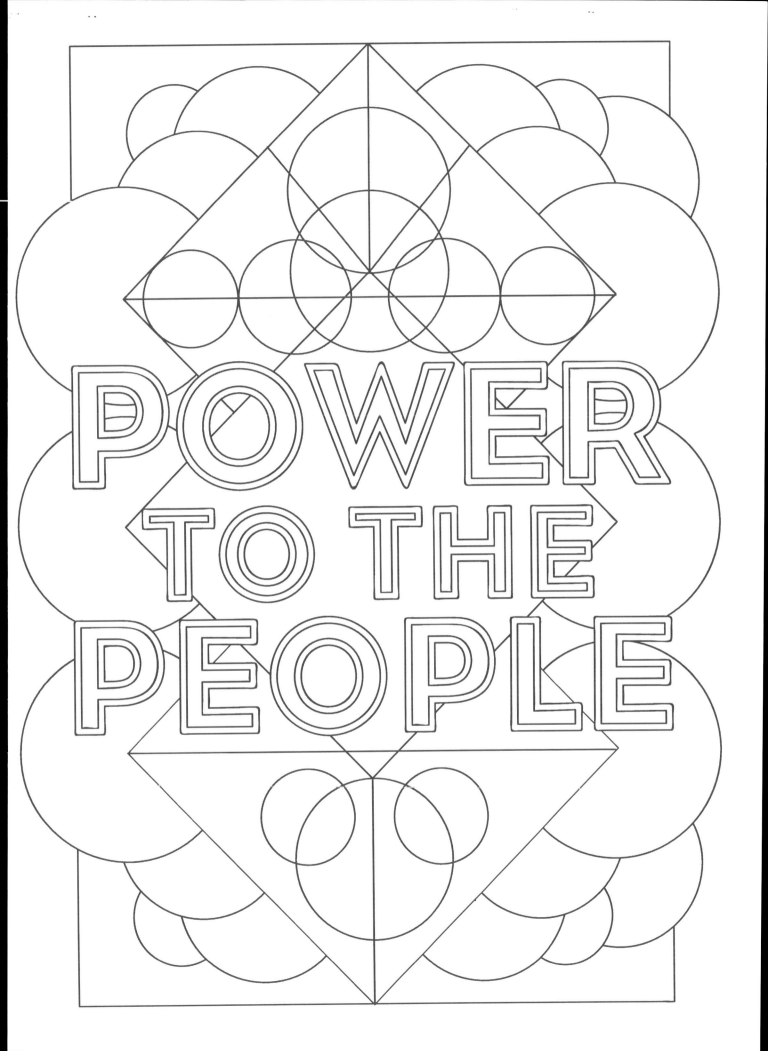

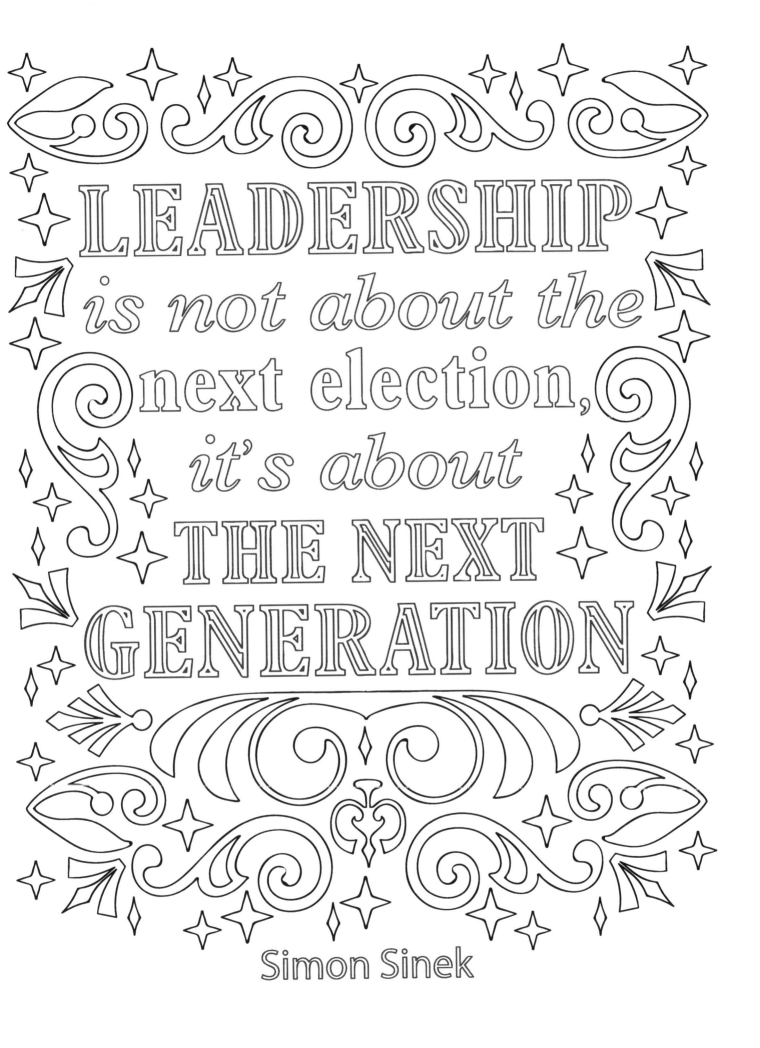

Made in the USA
San Bernardino, CA
14 December 2016